W9-BLW-992

The Bible

FOR YOUNG CHILDREN

Marie-Hélène Delval ✦ Götting

The Bible

FOR YOUNG CHILDREN

Eerdmans Books for Young Readers

Grand Rapids, Michigan ✦ Cambridge, U.K.

This selection of Bible stories, paraphrased for young readers, uses language and imagery appropriate for children while remaining faithful to the spirit of the biblical texts.

In the very beginning,
the world looked like nothing.
The day and the night
were all mixed together.
Then God said,
"LIGHT!"

God made the sky
with its sun and moon and stars.
God made the earth with its seas.
God made the trees grow,
and all the plants too.
It was beautiful!

God made the animals:
the very big ones
and the very small ones.
The ones that fly,
the ones that run,
the ones that crawl,
the ones that swim.
It was beautiful!

God gave the earth to men and women
and their children
so they could live there
and make it even more beautiful!

But then people became mean,
so mean that God was sorry
that he had given them the world.
He wanted to destroy everything he had made.
So God sent a flood
to wash it all away.

But there was Noah.
Noah loved God, and God loved Noah.
God told Noah to build an ark.
Noah brought two of every creature
from the earth
into this huge boat —
even the birds and the snakes.
Finally Noah went into the ark
with his wife and his children,
and God closed the door behind them.

It rained for forty days and forty nights.
Then the water slowly went away
and the earth dried out.
Noah left the ark with his family,
with the lions, the bears, the elephants,
the doves, and the snakes.
Among the gray clouds a colorful rainbow shone.
This was God's promise
that he would never, ever again
destroy the earth like this.

Abraham and Sarah were old
and they didn't have any children.
God said to Abraham,
"Can you count the stars in the night sky?
I promise you that
your children and grandchildren
will be like those stars —
so many that no one will be able to count them!"

The next spring,
Sarah gave birth to a baby boy.
She called him Isaac,
which means "God laughs."

Jacob was the son of Isaac.
One night, he had a dream.
He saw God's angels
walking on a ladder of light
that stretched from the earth to the sky.
And God said to Jacob,
"From now on, your new name will be Israel,
which means 'God is strong!'"

Life in Egypt was hard
for the children of Israel.
Pharaoh, the king of Egypt,
made them work like slaves.
Because there were so many Israelites,
Pharaoh ordered his soldiers
to kill the newborn babies.

One mother hid her baby in a basket
and placed it by the edge of a river.
Pharaoh's daughter found the basket.
She took the baby in her arms and said,
"Little one, you will be my son.
You will be a prince in Egypt!"
She called him Moses,
which means "saved from the water."

Moses grew up.
One day, in the desert,
he saw a burning bush.
The voice of God called to him from the fire,
"Moses, Moses!
My people are miserable.
Go and lead them out of Egypt!"

The Israelites finally escaped from Egypt.
Pharaoh sent his horses, chariots,
and riders after them.
But God divided the sea in two
and let the Israelites pass.
Then it closed up behind them,
swallowing the chariots of Pharaoh,
and all his horses and riders.

The Israelites arrived
at Mount Sinai,
the mountain of God.
Moses climbed the mountain,
and God spoke to him there.
God gave Moses his commandments
written on two stone tablets.

For forty years,
the Israelites walked in the desert.
At the end of this very long trip,
they came to the Promised Land,
the country that God gave them —
the sweet land of Canaan!

Samuel was a young boy.
One night, God called to him:
"Samuel! Samuel!"
The child answered:
"Speak, Lord, your servant is listening."
Samuel would become a prophet,
someone who speaks in the name of God.

God sent Samuel to Bethlehem,
to the house of Jesse,
a man who had seven sons.
The youngest was a shepherd named David.
God had chosen him
to become the king of Israel.
Samuel laid his hand on David and blessed him.

God's people were at war.
In the enemy army was a giant named Goliath.
The Israelite soldiers were afraid of him.
But little David said,
"I am not afraid — God is with me.
I will laugh at this giant!"
David threw a stone with his sling.
The stone hit Goliath in the forehead,
and Goliath fell to the ground!

King Solomon was the son of David.
One night, God spoke to him in a dream:
"Ask me for anything you want,
and I will give it to you."
Solomon answered:
"Lord, give me a heart that is wise,
so that I might be a good king!"
And God was happy with the answer.

King Solomon built a magnificent temple
for the Lord.
He put the stone tablets
that God gave to Moses
in the middle of the temple,
in a gold box.

There was a huge city called Nineveh.
One day, God said to the prophet Jonah,
"Go tell the people of Nineveh
that I am going to destroy their city
because they are very wicked!"
But Jonah was afraid to go to Nineveh.
He boarded a ship
to flee far away from God.

God sent a raging storm.
The ship was going to sink!
Jonah said to the sailors,
"God is angry. It is all my fault!
Throw me overboard!"
The sailors threw Jonah into the sea,
and immediately the storm stopped.
God sent a giant fish
to swallow Jonah.

Jonah stayed in the belly of the fish
for three days and three nights.
He prayed and he cried out,
"From the bottom of the sea,
from my deep despair,
bring me back, Lord!"
And God heard his prayer.

God told the giant fish
to spit Jonah out on the shore.
Then Jonah went to Nineveh.
The people listened to him
and promised not to do
wicked things anymore.
And God promised
not to destroy their city.

In the kingdom of Persia,
King Darius made a law
that anyone who prayed to God would be killed.
But Daniel still prayed in secret.
The king learned about it
and commanded that Daniel be thrown
into a pit full of hungry lions.

When the king came to look inside the pit,
he saw Daniel sitting with the lions.
The lions had not hurt him.
The king declared,
"God of Daniel, you are great!
There is no God greater than you!"
And the king had Daniel taken out of the pit.

Isaiah was a prophet.
He announced with joy,
"A baby will be born.
He will be a king,
and the Spirit of God will be with him.
Those who walk in the dark
will see a great light!"

This great king came —
the Son of God!
He was a baby,
born in a stable.
Mary was his mother,
and he was called Jesus.

The shepherds came to the stable
because an angel told them,
"The savior is born!
Come see!
There is great joy
on earth and in heaven!"

The wise men came
from a country far away
because a star led them to the stable.
They brought with them
gold, frankincense, and myrrh,
gifts for a king.

Jesus grew up in Nazareth,
where he lived with Joseph and Mary.
And God was with him.

When Jesus was grown up,
he walked along the roads of his country
with twelve of his friends.
Jesus said to everyone he met,
"Listen to the good news!
God loves you all!
You are his dear children!"

Jesus told a story:
"A shepherd had a hundred sheep.
One day, the smallest sheep was lost.
So the shepherd searched and searched
until he found the little sheep.
God is like this shepherd:
each one of his children is precious to him!"

People came from everywhere
to listen to Jesus.
He spoke to them and blessed them.
And when they were sick,
he healed them.

Many people loved Jesus.
When Jesus passed by,
they were happy. They called out,
"You are the Lord, the Son of God!
You are blessed, the one who comes
to bring us love and peace."

But there were other people
who were angry at Jesus.
Those people said,
"No one has the right
to say he is the Son of God!"
Those people wanted to kill him.

Jesus was condemned
and nailed to a cross.
Those who believed in him were so sad
that in their hearts
it was like night.

But in the morning
the light of God brightened
the hearts of those who were sad.
The love of God
was stronger than death:
Jesus had risen!

Jesus is alive forever!
Jesus is the light
that is stronger than the darkness!

To find the full text of the stories retold in
The Bible for Young Children:

This edition published in 2010 by
Eerdmans Books for Young Readers,
an imprint of William B. Eerdmans Publishing Co.
2140 Oak Industrial Dr. NE, Grand Rapids, Michigan 49505
P.O. Box 163, Cambridge CB3 9PU U.K.

www.eerdmans.com/youngreaders

Manufactured at Toppan Leefung Printing Ltd in Guangdong Province, China, February 2010, first printing

10 11 12 13 14 15 16 17   10 9 8 7 6 5 4 3 2 1

Library of Congress Cataloging-in-Publication Data

Delval, Marie-Hélène.
[Bible pour les tout-petits. English]
The Bible for young children / by Marie-Hélène Delval ; illustrated by Götting.
p. cm.
Includes bibliographical references and index.
ISBN 978-0-8028-5383-7 (alk. paper)
1. Bible stories, English. I. Götting, Jean-Claude, 1963- II. Title.
BS551.3.D44 2010
220.9'505—dc22
2010005164

Other books in this series:

Psalms for Young Children
Marie-Hélène Delval • Arno

Animals of the Bible for Young Children
Marie-Hélène Delval • Aurélia Fronty